SPECIALS
IN
STEAM

G.W.R. "Modified Hall" class 4-6-0 No. 6963 THROWLEY HALL enters Devizes with the LCGB "Wessex Downsman" rail tour on 4 April 1965, en route from Reading to Bristol.

[*Patrick Russell*]

SPECIALS
IN
STEAM

BRIAN STEPHENSON AND PATRICK RUSSELL

London
IAN ALLAN LTD

First published 1968
Third impression 1974

ISBN O 7110 0018 2

Printed and published in the United Kingdom by Ian Allan Ltd, Shepperton, Surrey

INTRODUCTION

It is safe to say that more railway photographs have been taken during the last ten years than throughout the whole previous history of railways. Not until its days were numbered did the steam locomotive attract the appreciative attention of thousands whose enthusiasm had hitherto remained unawakened.

During this period railway societies have thrived as never before, their memberships multiplying, their activities expanding. Foremost among these the rail tour has been by far the most popular. With the effects of first the Modernisation Plan and more recently the Beeching Plan really taking root, there has been no shortage of opportunities for the running of last trains on lines to be abandoned, or last journeys behind the last of the class.

Promoters of these excursions have often displayed remarkable ingenuity in planning itineraries and in providing interesting motive power. They have been tireless in their efforts to persuade the authorities to fall in with their schemes. In this way has it been possible to see "United States Lines" restart a heavy train on Shap unassisted and without losing its feet, thus has "Blue Peter" from Aberdeen stalled on Honiton incline, and thus has "Clun Castle" arrived at Newcastle upon Tyne.

It seems most likely that rail touring by enthusiasts first began back in September 1938. That was on the famous occasion when the Railway Correspondence and Travel Society took advantage of the L.N.E.R.'s restoration to working order of the veteran Stirling Single to run their own special train, complete with contemporary coaches, from Kings Cross to Peterborough.

Since the early nineteen fifties the vogue for rail touring has grown steadily in scope and ambition. Right from the start the Railway Correspondence and Travel Society, the Stephenson Locomotive Society and the Railway Enthusiasts Club of Farnborough have been pre-eminent among organisers. More recently they have been joined by the Locomotive Club of Great Britain. Highlight of 1953 was undoubtedly when the two G.N.R. Ivatt Atlantics were brought out of York Railway Museum to haul the privately sponsored Plant Centenarian excursions. The following year saw the start of the famous series of Farnborough Flyers from Doncaster. From 1955 and 1957 respectively the special trains run in connection with the Annual General Meetings of the Talyllyn and Festiniog Railway Preservation Societies have become regular annual events. Ian Allan Limited supported the rail tour scene with their popular series of Locospotters' Specials and other excursions. They have generally opted for the large type of motive power carefully selected to provide the maximum appeal.

As the withdrawal of steam locomotives developed in earnest from 1962, so did enthusiasm and the demand for rail tours reach a previously undreamed of level. The three foremost societies have all now run well over a hundred tours each, and successful tours have also been run by more than fifty other organisations. Inevitably some proposed tours have had to be cancelled, but others have proved so popular as to make a repeat journey necessary. During the last two or three years there has scarcely been a weekend without a tour of some kind, and on at least one occasion as many as six different ventures were planned for the very same day.

Today the steam locomotive has all but departed from the scene, and the veritable floodtide of tours is now beginning to show signs of receding. As steam is banned systematically region by region, the opportunities are rapidly shrinking, and the water and servicing problem becomes ever more paramount. A sentimental chapter in railway history of homage to a glorious era is about to close.

During the past twenty years well over five hundred specials in steam have been run. There is no doubt that every one of them will have been photographed hundreds of times by passengers, spectators and mobilised pursuers. We have seen thousands of these photographs, and present here a short representative selection of those we particularly like. Our criterion has always been to place quality of photograph before interest of subject matter, and in just over two hundred pictures it is quite impossible to show every special train. This book, therefore, does not attempt to represent itself as a comprehensive illustrated history of rail tours, or indeed any form of statistical record. The pictures are not arranged chronologically, nor are the trains grouped under their respective tour organisers. We have, however, made a conscious attempt to illustrate as many types of locomotive as possible, and to restrict common favourites from appearing too often. Our prime consideration has been in presentation and layout. We have tried to show the pictures on each page in the most pleasing possible way. Some order is of course essential, and our theme has taken us on a geographical tour of the British Isles. From time to time, however, we have broken our journey to intersperse features highlighting preserved locomotives.

Our gratitude and appreciation is due to all those fellow photographers who have supplied us so freely with examples of their work, and without whose friendly assistance there would inevitably have been far less variety in the final selection.

P. J. R.
B. W. L. S.
1968.

Early in 1938 the L.N.E.R. took the G.N.R. Stirling "Single" 4-2-2 No. 1 out of retirement from York Railway Museum and restored it to working order to haul a demonstration run from Kings Cross to Stevenage on 30 June that year, comparing the "Flying Scotsman" of 1888 with the A4 hauled train of 1938 to which passengers transferred on arrival at Stevenage. The carriages used were seven six-wheeled coaches reconditioned to form a typical East Coast Joint Stock formation of fifty years before. No. 1 was used again for a public excursion to Cambridge in August, and then in September the RCTS had the happy idea of using No. 1 for a special run to Peterborough before the veteran engine was returned to the museum.

No. 1 at Cambridge on 24 August 1938. 　　　　　[*Donovan Box*

STIRLING SINGLE

Patrick Stirling's first eight-foot single-drivered 4-2-2 No. 1 of 1870 passes Ganwick with the RCTS special from Kings Cross to Peterborough on 11 September 1938.

[*M. W. Earley*

IVATT ATLANTICS

The last G.N.R. class C1 4-4-2 to remain in service, No. 62822 awaits departure from Kings Cross on its final run to Doncaster with British Railways' "Ivatt Atlantic Special" in the foggy gloom of 26 November 1950.

[W. J. Reynolds

THE PLANT CENTENARIAN

To celebrate the centenary in 1953 of Doncaster Locomotive Works, known locally as the "Plant", the two preserved G.N.R. Ivatt Atlantics — small-boilered class C2 4-4-2 No. 990 HENRY OAKLEY and large-boilered class C1 4-4-2 No. 251 — were brought out from retirement in York Railway Museum to haul two special trains privately sponsored by Messrs. H. T. S. Bailey, A. F. Pegler and L. J. W. Smith.

No. 990 HENRY OAKLEY & No. 251 climb Holloway bank soon after departure from Kings Cross with "The Plant Centenarian" for Doncaster on 20 September 1953.

[R. E. Vincent

A going-away shot of HENRY OAKLEY climbing Holloway bank.

[R. E. Vincent

The two atlantics storm through Great Ponton cutting on the climb to Stoke Tunnel with the second "Plant Centenarian" from Leeds to Kings Cross, 27 September 1953.

[P. H. Wells

L.N.E.R. class J50/4 0-6-0T No. 68987 approaches Ludgate Hill on the climb from Snow Hill and the Metropolitan widened lines with the RCTS "London & North Kent" rail tour on the way from Finsbury Park to Blackfriars, 21 March 1959.

[*R. C. Riley*]

G.N.R. TANK ENGINES

G.N.R. class C12 4-4-2T No. 67357 at Stamford with the Railway Enthusiasts' Club "Charnwood Forester", 14 April 1957. The train is crossing from the G.N.R. Essendine branch to the Midland Peterborough–Leicester line.

[*P. H. Wells*]

L.N.E.R. class A1/1 4-6-2 No. 60113 GREAT NORTHERN entering York prior to the return journey to Kings Cross with the B.R. "Great Northern Centenary Special", 16 July 1950. This train was run to commemorate the opening of the line throughout from Maiden Lane (London) to York.

[J. C. Flemons

L.N.E.R. class A4 4-6-2 No. 60007 SIR NIGEL GRESLEY accelerates past Wood Green on 28 September 1952 with the privately sponsored "Centenaries Express", commemorating the opening of the direct route from Kings Cross to York. [C. R. L. Coles

GREAT NORTHERN CENTENARIES

FLYING SCOTSMAN

The privately preserved L.N.E.R. class A3 4-6-2 No. 4472 FLYING SCOTSMAN reaches the summit of the climb between Huddersfield and Manchester at Stand-edge Tunnel with a Gainsborough Model Railway Society excursion from Doncaster to Llandudno on 4 June 1966.

[Brian Stephenson

⋀

FLYING SCOTSMAN heads south from Leamington Spa with the ''Farnborough Flyer'', 12 September 1964. The owner of 4472, Mr. Alan Pegler, has been closely associated with the organization over the years of the specials to the Farnborough Air Display.   [R. J. Blenkinsop

FLYING SCOTSMAN, now fitted with two tenders, speeds towards Welwyn Viaduct with the Altrinchamian Railway Excursion Society ''Elizabethan'' special from Kings Cross on 22 October 1966.   [Brian Stephenson
⋁

GREAT EASTERN

G.E.R. class J15 0-6-0 No. 65476 storms out of Epping with the repeat LCGB "Great Eastern Suburban" rail tour of 28 April 1962, bound for Ongar. *[Patrick Russell*

The last G.E.R. class E4 2-4-0 No. 62785 gathers speed after leaving the Cambridge—Liverpool Street main line at Shelford with a Cambridge University Railway Club engine driving special bound for Bartlow and Haverhill on 5 May 1959.   [*W. J. V. Anderson*

G.E.R. class J15 0-6-0 No. 65443 pauses at Inworth with an R.E.C. open wagon special over the remains of the Tollesbury light railway from Kelvedon to Tiptree on 6 April 1957.   [*R. C. Riley*

Class N7/4 0-6-2T No. 69621 prepares to leave Liverpool Street for Palace Gates on the first leg of the repeat LCGB "Great Eastern Suburban" rail tour, 28 April 1962.   [*Brian Stephenson*

G.E.R. TANK ENGINES

Class J68 0-6-0T No. 68646 couples on to the RCTS "London River" rail tour at Blackheath before running to Liverpool Street via New Cross and the Thames Tunnel, 29 March 1958. The train had come from Angerstein Wharf behind S.E.C.R. class H 0-4-4T No. 31518 which can be seen at the far end.

[*J. Spencer Gilks*

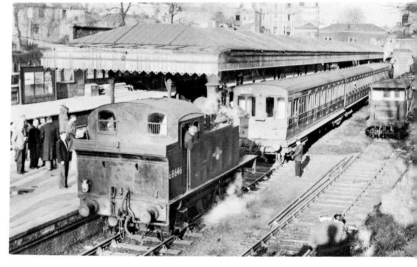

The gleaming Liverpool Street station pilot, class N7/4 0-6-2T No. 69614 waits at Gospel Oak with the RCTS "Hertfordshire No. 2" rail tour on 27 April 1958.
[*J. Spencer Gilks*

G.E.R. "Claud Hamilton" ≫ class D16/3 4-4-0 No. 62567 waiting to depart from Bishopsgate goods depot with the RCTS "East Anglian" special to Marks Tey on 6 September 1953.   [J. G. Dewing

A panoramic view showing No. 62567 departing from Bishopsgate with the same train. Both the East London line to New Cross and the main line from Liverpool Street are visible on the far left of the picture. [R. E. Vincent
∨

BISHOPSGATE

PACIFICS ON THE GREAT CENTRAL

ABOVE: L.M.S. "Coronation" class 4-6-2 No. 46251 CITY OF NOTTINGHAM leaves Catesby Tunnel with the RCTS "East Midlander No. 7" on 9 May 1964, whilst running from Nottingham Victoria to Didcot. *[M. Pope*

UPPER RIGHT: L.N.E.R. class A3 4-6-2 No. 60103 FLYING SCOTSMAN sets out from Leicester Central with an Ian Allan Locospotters Club special from Marylebone to Doncaster on 21 April 1960. *[C. P. Walker*

LOWER RIGHT: S.R. "Merchant Navy" class 4-6-2 No. 35030 ELDER DEMPSTER LINES climbs towards Chorleywood with the LCGB "Great Central" rail tour from Waterloo to Nottingham Victoria on 3 September 1966. This was the day before complete closure of the Great Central main line between Calvert and Rugby.

[Brian Stephenson

≪The last G.C.R. class J11/3 0-6-0 No. 64354 stands at Egginton Junction between Derby Friargate and Burton-on-Trent with the LCGB ''Midland Limited'' rail tour from Nottingham Victoria, 14 October 1962.

[Brian Stephenson

Another view of the LCGB ''Midland Limited'' rail tour on 14 October 1962 before departure from Marylebone for Nottingham Victoria, behind L.N.E.R. class B16/2 4-6-0 No. 61438.
∨
[Brian Stephenson

GREAT CENTRAL

G.C.R. class 04/1 2-8-0 ≫ No. 63585 takes the sharp curve of the Sheffield line as it leaves Retford on 12 October 1963 with a Gainsborough Model Railway Society special.
[T. G. Hepburn

L.N.E.R. class B1 4-6-0s Nos. 61173 & 61131 approach New Hucknall Sidings with the LCGB "Great Central" rail tour on the Nottingham Victoria to Elsecar Junction part of the journey, 3 September 1966.
∨ *[Patrick Russell*

THE PENNINE PULLMAN

The Ian Allan Trains Illustrated "Pennine Pullman" of 12 May 1956 was hauled between Ashburys and Shef-field Victoria via the Calder Valley main line and Barnsley by two G.C.R. "Director" class D11 4-4-0s Nos. 62662 PRINCE OF WALES & 62664 PRINCESS MARY. They are seen below crossing the Rochdale Canal at the approach to Todmorden as they drift down from Summit Tunnel.

[W. A. Corkhill]

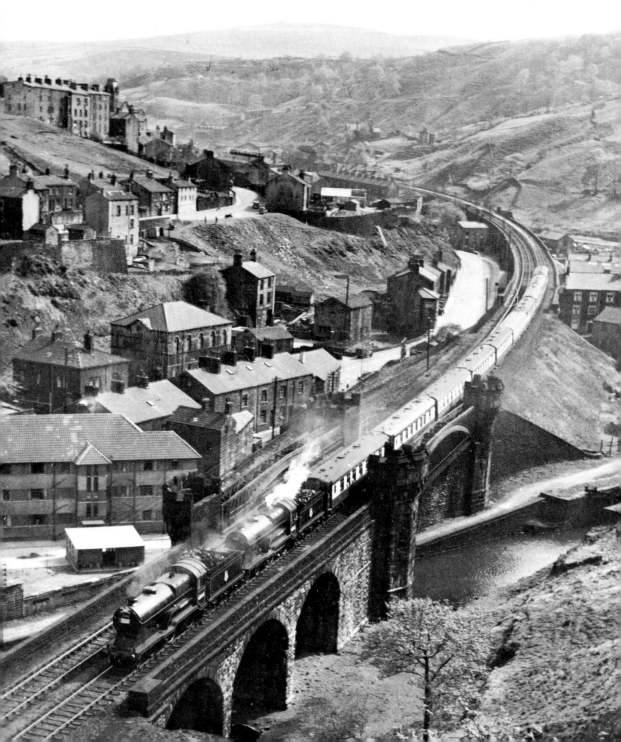

Another view of the "Pennine Pullman" shows the immaculate "Directors" approaching Luddendenfoot.

[B. K. B. Green

The two "Directors" take water from Luddendenfoot troughs as they head for Sowerby Bridge Tunnel.

[Eric Oldham

SIR NIGEL GRESLEY

The A4 Preservation Society purchased No. 4498 from B.R. in 1966. During 1967 the Society used it for several excursions in different parts of the country.

UPPER LEFT: L.N.E.R. class A4 4-6-2 No. 4498 SIR NIGEL GRESLEY tops Grayrigg bank on its inaugural run from Crewe to Carlisle on 1 April 1967.
[Brian Stephenson]

LOWER LEFT: SIR NIGEL GRESLEY crosses the Forth Bridge returning from Aberdeen to Glasgow Central on 20 May 1967. [John R. P. Hunt]

In June No. 4498 was used ▷ for two excursions on the Southern Region. On the first trip SIR NIGEL GRESLEY passes through Woking cutting en route from Waterloo to Bournemouth on 3 June 1967.

[*Patrick Russell*

During the first leg of a triangular tour, Leeds–Carlisle–Newcastle–Leeds, No. 4498 streaks across Arten Gill Viaduct as it makes for Dent and Ais Gill, 27 August 1967 ⱽ

[*Patrick Russell*

N.E.R. class J72 0-6-0T No. 69023 JOEM built by B.R. at Darlington in 1951 and now on the Keighley & Worth Valley line, propels the K.W.V.R. "Centenary Special" into Keighley on 13 April 1967. [G. W. Morrison

WEST RIDING

L.N.E.R. class A1 4-6-2 No. 60157 GREAT EASTERN passes Marsh Lane on the approach to Leeds City with the Ian Allan Trains Illustrated "Pennine Limited" from Kings Cross, 26 April 1958.   [J. K. Morton

WD class 2-8-0 No. 90348 ▷ waits to leave Darlington Bank Top with the RCTS "East Midlander No. 5" on 13 May 1962 for the short journey to North Road. [*Patrick Russell*]

English-Electric type 3 diesel-electric Co-Co No. D6769 crosses the East Coast main line on the level at the S. & D. Crossing with the RCTS "Blythe & Tyne" rail tour on 19 September 1965. This train is traversing the route of the Stockton & Darlington Railway, the diesel having replaced class A4 4-6-2 No. 60004 WILLIAM WHITELAW at Eaglescliffe for the journey to North Road, due to last minute restrictions on the pacific. ▽ [*Patrick Russell*]

DARLINGTON

The privately preserved L.N.E.R. class K4 2-6-0 No. 3442 THE GREAT MARQUESS heads out of Bishop Auckland with the RCTS ''North Eastern No. 2'' rail tour bound for Relly Mill and Newcastle Central on 10 April 1965.

[*G. W. Morrison*

THE GREAT MARQUESS

No. 3442 comes round the curve from Preston Park to Hove with a Locomotive Preservation (Sussex) Ltd., special from Victoria to Southampton, 12 March 1967. The bell fitted to the ''K4'' was presented to Lord Garnock, owner of THE GREAT MARQUESS, by the motive power department of the Pennsylvania Railroad. The bell had originally been fitted to one of the famous Pennsy ''K4'' pacifics.

[*Brian Stephenson*

THE GREAT MARQUESS and L.N.E.R. class A3 4-6-2 No. 4472 FLYING SCOTSMAN leave Harrogate with the combined train of two Ian Allan specials to Darlington, one with No. 4472 from Kings Cross and the other with No. 3442 from Leeds, 3 October 1964.
[Mrs. Michaeles Stephenson

THE GREAT MARQUESS storms up the 1 in 90 past Chinley North Junction soon after taking over the Middleton Railway Trust's ''Derbyshire Dawdler'' at Chinley for the journey to Derby via Peak Forest on 22 April 1967.
[Brian Stephenson

≪N.E.R. class Q7 0-8-0 No. 63460 passes Wellfield with the RCTS "North Eastern Limited" on 2 May 1964. [G. W. Morrison

"The Tyne Docker". B.R. standard class 9F 2-10-0 No. 92063 takes the Biddick Lane line at South Pelaw Junction with iron ore empties from Consett to Tyne Dock on 19 November 1966. This was the last steam hauled iron ore train and conveyed an extra brakevan for enthusiasts. It was also the last train to use the Biddick Lane route. [Ian S. Carr ⋁

CO. DURHAM

L.N.E.R. class V3 2-6-2T No. 67620 passes Jesmond on the way to Ponteland with the RCTS—SLS ''North Eastern Tour'' from Newcastle Central, 29 September 1963.

[*M. Brian Rutherford*

L.M.S. Ivatt class 4MT 2-6-0 No. 43057 crosses the Ouseburn Viaduct soon after leaving Newcastle Central for the Riverside line on the RCTS ''Blythe & Tyne'' rail tour on 19 September 1965.   [*Patrick Russell*

TYNESIDE

ALSTON BRANCH

L.M.S. Ivatt class 4MT 2-6-0 No. 43121 passes Lambley
on its way from Haltwhistle to Alston with the Branch
Line Society–Scottish Locomotive Preservation Society
"Scottish Rambler", 26 March 1967.   [*Robin Vallance*

NATIONAL COAL BOARD

N.C.B. Northumberland Area 0-6-0T No. 39 waits at Lyne-mouth before returning to Ashington with the Stephenson Locomotive Society—Manches-ter Locomotive Society "Ashing-ton" rail tour on 10 June 1967.

[*Ian S. Carr*

N.C.B. Swansea Area 0-4-0ST GRAIG MERTHYR makes the return journey from Graig Merthyr Colliery to Pontardulais with a Warwickshire Railway Society tour on 8 July 1967.

[*Patrick Russell*

N.C.B. West Ayr Area 0-6-0T No. 17 with a Branch Line Society brakevan special at Minnivey Mine on 20 March 1965.   [*Derek Cross*

L.N.E.R. class J38 0-6-0 No. 65914 returns from Menstrie to Alloa with the BLS–SLPS Easter "Scottish Rambler" on 11 April 1966.

[Patrick Russell

SCOTLAND – I

L.N.E.R. class A2 4-6-2 No. 60527 SUN CHARIOT departs from Broughty Ferry for Glasgow with the SLS–BLS Easter "Scottish Rambler" on 28 March 1964.

[G. W. Morrison

L.N.E.R. class K4 2-6-0 No. 61995 CAMERON OF LOCHIEL stops at Crianlarich Upper for water with the SLS "White Cockade" special returning from Fort William to Glasgow on 18 June 1960. [W. J. V. Anderson

N.B.R. class J36 0-6-0 No. 65288 approaches Kincardine along the sea wall of the Firth of Forth with the Railway Society of Scotland "Fife & Clackmannanshire" rail tour, 22 October 1966. [David C. Smith

The preserved N.B.R. "Glen" class 4-4-0 No. 256 GLEN DOUGLAS crosses the Forth Bridge to North Queensferry with the SLS–BLS Easter "Scottish Rambler" on 30 March 1964.

[W. J. V. Anderson

GLEN DOUGLAS pilots N.B.R. class J37 0-6-0 No. 64632 as they climb away from Bridge of Orchy past Loch Tulla with the SLS "Jacobite" rail tour to Fort William and Mallaig on 1 June 1963.

[W. J. V. Anderson

GLEN DOUGLAS

GLEN DOUGLAS climbs Dalgetty bank with the RCTS "Fife Coast" rail tour from Glasgow St. Enoch to Leuchars Junction via Edinburgh Waverley, 28 August 1965.
[Patrick Russell

Later the same afternoon GLEN DOUGLAS rejoined the "Fife Coast" rail tour at Thornton Junction to take the train to Perth via Ladybank and Newburgh and is seen approaching Bridge of Earn. This proved to be the last occasion Glen Douglas hauled a special before being placed in the Glasgow Museum of Transport. [Brian Stephenson

HIGHLAND RAILWAY "JONES GOODS"

The preserved H.R. Jones Goods 4-6-0 No. 103 climbs from Greenock Princes Pier past Port Glasgow on 17 April 1965 with the SLS–BLS Easter "Scottish Rambler" heading for East Kilbride.

[W. J. V. Anderson

LOWER LEFT: No. 103 passes Beattock Summit with a Branch Line Society tour returning from Lockerbie to Glasgow during its final run before retirement to the Glasgow Museum of Transport, 17 October 1965. [*W. J. V. Anderson*

The Jones Goods climbs the 1 in 80 from Dunkeld to Kingswood Tunnel whilst working over the Highland main line from Inverness to Perth with the SLS—RCTS ''Scottish Rail Tour'' on 15 June 1960. [*W. J. V. Anderson*

≪ The preserved C.R. 4-2-2 No. 123 gets the road into Perth with an SLS special to Crieff, 11 October 1958. The train comprises of the two restored "Caley" coaches. [W. J. V. Anderson

No. 123 and N.B.R. "Glen" class 4-4-0 No. 256 GLEN DOUGLAS depart from Oban with an SLS special returning to Glasgow on 12 May 1962. [G. W. Morrison
∀

CALEDONIAN RAILWAY No. 123

No. 123 passes Shotts with the SLS–BLS Easter "Scottish Rambler" en route from Glasgow Central to Edinburgh Princes Street, 19 April 1965.
[*Paul Riley*

The "Caley Single" on the Southern piloting L.S.W.R. class T9 4-4-0 No. 120 near Balcombe with a "Blue Belle" special returning to Victoria on 15 September 1963.
[*Brian Stephenson*

GORDON HIGHLANDER

The preserved G.N.S.R. class F 4-4-0 No. 49 GORDON HIGHLANDER departs from Glasgow Central on 19 April 1965 with the SLS–BLS Easter "Scottish Rambler" to Edinburgh Waverley.

[Eric Oldham

GORDON HIGHLANDER▷
approaches Wartle on the
Macduff branch with the
SLS–RCTS "Scottish
Rail Tour", 13 June 1960.
[W. J. V. Anderson

GORDON HIGHLANDER
pilots H.R. Jones Goods
4-6-0 No. 103 on the
climb to Slochd Summit
from the south with the
RCTS–SLS "Scottish
Rail Tour" on 14 June
1962. [W. J. V. Anderson
▽

C. R. Pickersgill 4-4-0 No. 54485 curves towards Methven on the short branch from Methven Junction with the SLS – RCTS "Scottish Rail Tour" from Perth on 15 June 1960.   [W. J. V. Anderson]

SCOTLAND – II

N.B.R. class J37 0-6-0 No. 64569 crosses the River Eden at Guard Bridge with the RCTS "Fife Coast" rail tour as it makes for St. Andrews and the Fife coast line to Thornton Junction, 28 August 1965.   [Brian Stephenson]

L.M.S. Hughes/Fowler "Crab" 2-6-0 No. 42739 crosses Gadgirth Viaduct near Annbank with an SLS brake-van tour of Ayrshire branch lines, 16 April 1965. *[Derek Cross*

L.N.E.R. class B1 4-6-0 No. 61342 near Killochan in the Girvan Valley with the BLS - SLPS Easter "Scottish Rambler" returning from Girvan en route to Muirkirk on 10 April 1966. *[Patrick Russell*

G.S. & W.R. class D11 4-4-0 No. 301 waits to depart from Dublin West-land Row with an Irish Railway Record Society special to Rosslare on 9 September 1960. [*L. King*

The restored G.S. & W.R. 101 class 0-6-0 No. 184 takes water at Kildare whilst hauling an IRRS special from Dublin Amiens Street to Ballylinan, 9 July 1960.
[*S. C. Nash*

CORAS IOMPAIR EIREANN

G.S. & W.R. class J15 0-6-0 No. 194 waits to leave Glanmire Road Station with the IRRS St. Patrick's Day rail tour from Dublin to Youghal, 17 March 1962. *[J. G. Dewing*

CORK

C.B.S.C.R. class B4 4-6-0T No. 464 crosses one of the bridges over the River Lee on the Cork City line en route from Glanmire Road to Albert Quay during the IRRS St. Patrick's Day rail tour, 17 March 1961. *[J. G. Dewing*

The preserved G.N.R. (I) class S 4-4-0 No. 171 SLIEVE GULLION waits to leave Larne on the return journey to Belfast York Road with a Railway Preservation Society of Ireland special on 8 October 1966.　　　[*L. King*

GREAT NORTHERN 4-4-0s

G.N.R. (I) class V 3-cylinder compound 4-4-0 No. 85 MERLIN on arrival at Dundalk with the IRRS - SLS - RCTS "Irish Rail Tour" during the run from Dublin to Belfast, 9 June 1961. Standing on the right is N.C.C. class WT 2-6-4T No. 55.　　　[*S. C. Nash*

N.C.C. class U2 4-4-0 No. 74 DUNLUCE CASTLE on arrival at Antrim with the IRRS - SLS - RCTS "Irish Rail Tour" from Belfast York Road via Greenisland on 10 June 1961. DUNLUCE CASTLE is now preserved in the Belfast Transport Museum. *[L. King*

ULSTER

The G.S. & W.R. class J15 0-6-0 No. 186 preserved by the RPSI pilots N.C.C. class WT 2-6-4T No. 55 at Culley-backey with the RPSI "Dalriada" rail tour from Ballymena to Portrush, 13 May 1967. *[J. G. Dewing*

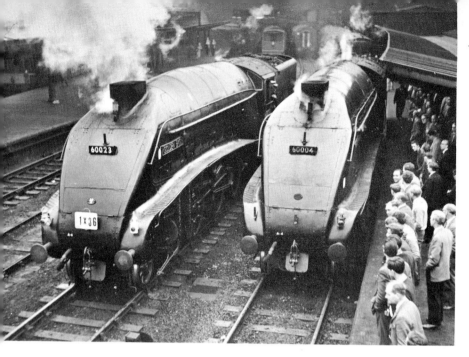

L.N.E.R. Class A4 4-6-2 No. 60023 GOLDEN EAGLE waits in the centre road at Citadel station to take over the RCTS "Three Summits" rail tour from sister engine No. 60004 WILLIAM WHITELAW for the return to Leeds via Shap and Ingleton, 30 June 1963.

[Patrick Russell

N.E.R. class J21 0-6-0 No. 65033 makes a vigorous departure from Carlisle with the RCTS–Stockton & Darlington Locomotive Society "J21" special on the return journey to Darlington via Penrith and Stainmore, 6 May 1960.

[Walter I. O. Moffat

VISITORS TO CARLISLE

L.N.E.R. class B1 4-6-0 No. 61278 of Dundee departs for Edinburgh via the Waverley route with the BR Scottish Region "B1 Farewell" excursion on 3 December 1966.
[Ian S. Carr

S.R. "Merchant Navy" class 4-6-2 No. 35012 UNITED STATES LINES moves forward from the centre road at Citadel station to take over the RCTS "Solway Ranger" rail tour for the return to Leeds via Ais Gill, 12 June 1964.
[Patrick Russell

A light sprinkling of snow lies on the fells as L.M.S. Stanier class 5MT 4-6-0 No. 45018 storms up Shap unaided in place of a failed ''Britannia'' pacific on a WRS Birmingham to Carlisle special, 28 November 1964.

[*Maurice S. Burns*

CROSSING THE FELLS

L.M.S. ''Coronation'' class 4-6-2 No. 46238 CITY OF CARLISLE leaves Shotlock Hill Tunnel between Garsdale and Ais Gill with the RCTS - SLS ''North Eastern Tour'' on 27 September 1963.

[*M. Brian Rutherford*

L.M.S. "Royal Scot" class 4-6-0 No. 46115 SCOTS GUARDSMAN pounds up to Ribblehead on the last two to Blea Moor Tunnel with the RCTS "Rebuilt Scot Commemorative" rail tour from Crewe to Carlisle, 13 February 1965. *[G. W. Morrison*

L.M.S. "Jubilee" class 4-6-0 No. 45562 ALBERTA ascends Grayrigg bank with the Jubilee Locomotive Preservation Society's "Border Countryman" from Leeds to Beattock on 25 February 1967. *[A. G. Cattle*

MIDLAND 4-4-0s

The preserved M.R. 3-cylinder compound 4-4-0 No. 1000 crosses the Goyt viaduct near Marple with an SLS Special from Birmingham to Gorton Works on 26 June 1960.

[Eric Oldham

UPPER RIGHT: L.M.S. class 2P 4-4-0 No. 40646 awaits departure from Birmingham New Street with an SLS special for Bedford via Leamington Spa and Northampton on 14 April 1962. [G. W. Morrison

The last M.R. 3P 4-4-0 No. 40726 at Manchester Central before departure with the SLS–MLS ''Hull & Barnsley'' special to Cudworth via the Hope Valley line on 24 August 1952. [Eric Oidham

B. R.
STANDARD
PACIFICS

"Britannia" class 4-6-2 No. 70038 ROBIN HOOD climbs past Slaithwaite with an SLS special returning from York to Birmingham on 2 July 1967. [D. Ian Wood

"Britannia" class 4-6-2 No. 70015 APOLLO storms the 1 in 80 gradient to Copy Pit Summit past Portsmouth with the RCTS "Lancastrian" rail tour on 19 March 1967. [G. W. Morrison

"Clan" class 4-6-2 No. 72007 CLAN MACKINTOSH proceeds cautiously along the Lancaster goods line with the RCTS "Ribble-Lune" rail tour, 23 May 1964. [G. W. Morrison

The unique class 8P 4-6-2 No. 71000 DUKE OF GLOUCESTER accelerates past Basford Hall Sidings soon after leaving Crewe with the Ian Allan Trains Illustrated "Pennine Limited" returning to Euston on 26 April 1958. [R. J. Blenkinsop

≪L.M.S. Hughes/Fowler class 5 2-6-0 No. 42942 drifts downgrade through Cleckheaton with the LCGB "Crab Commemorative" rail tour from Liverpool to Wakefield on 8 October 1966.
[Brian Stephenson

L.M.S. Hughes/Fowler class 5 2-6-0 No. 42727 runs wrongline past Connah's Quay power station on its way from Chester to Llandudno Junction with an SLS special from Birmingham, 27 March 1966.
[Brian Stephenson
∨

CRAB FAREWELL

Aspinall 2-4-2T No. 50647 and 0-6-0 No. 52438 charge the 1 in 27 gradient of the celebrated Werneth Incline with the SLS—MLS "Old Manchester" rail tour on 12 May 1956. *[J. Davenport*

L. & Y.R. ENGINES

The last Hughes 4-6-0 No. 50455 pauses at Manchester Victoria during an SLS tour from Blackpool to York, 1 July 1951.

The last Aspinall 0-6-0 No. 52515 and L.M.S. class 4F 0-6-0 No. 44408 at Sowerby Bridge before departing for Darlington with the Halifax Railfans Club "South Yorkshireman" tour on 29 September 1962. *[G. W. Morrison*

Class G2a 0-8-0 No. 49361 passes East Cannock Junction with an SLS tour of Midland mineral lines on 22 June 1963.

[J. B. Bucknall

L.N.W.R. SURVIVORS

The last Webb "Coal Tank" 0-6-2T No. 58926 and class G2a 0-8-0 No. 49121 stand in Ebbw Vale High Level station with the SLS special last train over the L.N.W.R. Abergavenny Junction to Merthyr line on 5 January 1958.

[J. D. Mills

The last M.R. class 4F 0-6-0 No. 43953 sets off from Burton-on-Trent past Horninglow Bridge with the RCTS "Midland Locomotives Requiem" rail tour from Nuneaton Abbey Street on 16 October 1965.

[Patrick Russell

MIDLAND SURVIVOR

The same train climbs to Kirkby South Tunnel on its way to Mansfield and Staveley Town. The last survivor, No. 43953, was built by Armstrong Whitworth and had been summoned from as far away as Workington to haul this train.

[Patrick Russell

◁ Class J94 0-6-0STs Nos. 68012 & 68006 storm flat-out up the lower part of the famous Hopton Incline in order to surmount the final stretch at 1 in 14 with the SLS "Cromford & High Peak Farewell" special on the last day of operation, 30 April 1967.

[*Brian Stephenson*

⋀
The same train restarts from Longcliffe after a lengthy stop for the saddle-tanks to replenish their water supply from the two old tenders on the right of the picture.

[*Patrick Russell*

The two J94s swing away from the Buxton–Ashbourne line as they leave Parsley Hay with the last day special returning to Middleton Top. A further special was run over the C.& H.P. line the same day in connection with an Anglo-Norse society excursion.

[*Patrick Russell*
⋁

≪ Stanier class 2P 0-4-4T No. 41901 stands at St. Albans Abbey station with the RCTS "Hertfordshire No. 2" rail tour after arrival from Watford Junction, 27 April 1958.
[J. G. Dewing]

Fowler class 4MT 2-6-4T No. 42343 passes Black Bull with the Manchester University Railway Society "Staffordshire Potter" on 13 March 1965 during a tour of N.S.R. lines.
[G. W. Morrison]
∨

L.M.S. TANK ENGINES

△
The preserved L.T. & S.R. 4-4-2T No. 80 THUNDERSLEY at Westcliff-on-Sea with the RCTS ''Southend Centenary Special'' from Bishopsgate on 11 February 1956.
[*J. G. Dewing*

N.L.R. 0-6-0T No. 58859 at Millwall with the LCGB ''Poplar & Edgware'' rail tour from Broad Street, 5 May 1956.
▽
[*S. C. Nash*

S.R. "Schools" class 4-4-0 No. 30925 CHELTENHAM and L.M.S. class 2P 4-4-0 No. 40646 await departure from Nottingham Victoria for Darlington with the RCTS "East Midlander No. 5" on 13 May 1962.

[Patrick Russell

L.N.E.R. class A2 4-6-2 No. 60532 BLUE PETER on Honiton incline shortly before stalling with the LCGB "A2 Commemorative" rail tour from Waterloo to Exeter, 14 August 1966.

[Brian Stephenson

LOCOMOTIVE EXCHANGE

L.M.S. "Coronation" ⋟ class 4-6-2 No. 46245 CITY OF LONDON sets out from Doncaster with a Home Counties Railway Society special returning to Kings Cross on 9 June 1963. [*Eric Oldham*]

The privately preserved G.W.R. "Castle" class 4-6-0 No. 7029 CLUN CASTLE leaves Kings Cross with an Ian Allan rail tour to Leeds on 17 September 1967.
⋁ [*Patrick Russell*]

G.W.R. "Modified Hall" class 4-6-0 No. 7929 WYKE HALL assists B.R. "Clan" class 4-6-2 No. 72008 CLAN MACLEOD with a Derbyshire Railway Society special from Leeds to Tyseley, Wolverhampton and Crewe seen approaching Swan Village, 24 March 1963.

[G. England

WEST MIDLANDS

G.W.R. 56XX class 0-6-2T No. 6697 passes Hockley soon after leaving Birmingham Snow Hill with an SLS special to Chester on 27 March 1966.

[Brian Stephenson

G.W.R. "Manor" class 4-6-0 No. 7827 LYDHAM MANOR pilots the privately preserved G.W.R. 45XX class 2-6-2T No. 4555 near Corwen on the journey from Ruabon to Towyn on 26 September with the 1964 Talyllyn Railway Preservation Society special. [M. Pope

The privately preserved G.W.R. "Castle" class 4-6-0 No. 7029 CLUN CASTLE crosses Chirk Viaduct into Wales with the LCGB "Severn & Dee" rail tour from Wolverhampton High Level to Chester on 26 February 1967. [Brian Stephenson

WELSH BORDERS

CONWAY VALLEY

On 24 September 1966 the LCGB ran their "Conway Valley" rail tour from Euston to North Wales. The highlight was undoubtedly the run up the Conway Valley from Llandudno Junction to Bettws-y-Coed and Blaenau Ffestiniog behind two L.M.S. stanier class 4MT 2-6-4Ts Nos. 42574 & 42644. Below: The train emerges from the 2 mile 388 yards long Festiniog Tunnel into the strange world of slate at Blaenau Ffestiniog.

[Brian Stephenson

Returning from Blaenau Ffestiniog the two tank engines coast downgrade from the Festiniog Tunnel past Roman Bridge in the valley of the Afon Lledr.

[Brian Stephenson

LOWER RIGHT: Back along the shore of the River Conway the train is seen again between Taly-y-Cafn and Glan Conway returning to Llandudno.

[Brian Stephenson

L.S.W.R. class T9 4-4-0 ≫ No. 30304 takes water at Welshpool before continuing to Towyn as pilot to G.W.R. "Dukedog" 4-4-0 No. 9027 with the first of the annual Talyllyn Railway Preservation Society specials on 24 September 1955.

[T. E. Williams

S.E.C.R. class D 4-4-0 No. 31075 pilots the last "Dean Goods" 0-6-0 No. 2538 from Shrewsbury on the westbound climb to Talerddig with the 1956 TRPS special on 22 September.   [T. E. Williams

∨

CAMBRIAN

G.W.R. 56XX class 0-6-2T No. 6656 passes under the now demolished Crumlin Viaduct with an SLS special on 6 May 1962 marking the closure to passengers of the Eastern and Western Valley lines from Newport the previous weekend.

[E. T. Gill]

G.W.R. 64XX class 0-6-0PT No. 6423 takes water at Llantrisant after running to Tondu and back with an SLS special formed of two Taff Vale railmotor trailers, 12 July 1952.

[R. C. Riley]

The celebrated G.W.R. "City" class 4-4-0 No. 3440 CITY OF TRURO pilots G.W.R. 43XX class 2-6-0 No. 4358 on the Ian Allan Trains Illustrated "Daffodil Express" at Hafodyrynys between Pontypool Road and Crumlin high level on 18 May 1957.

[*T. E. Williams*

CITY OF TRURO makes a fine display as it storms Hatton bank with an SLS special returning from Swindon to Birmingham Snow Hill on 16 June 1957.

[*T. E. Williams*

CITY OF TRURO

CITY OF TRURO pilots the preserved Midland "Compound" 4-4-0 No. 1000 as they leave Doncaster for Kings Cross on 20 April 1960 with an Ian Allan Locospotters Club special.

[Eric Oldham

L.M.S. 3-cylinder compound 4-4-0 No. 41123 surmounts Hatton bank with 1958 TRPS special which it hauled from Paddington to Shrewsbury on 27 September.

[*T. E. Williams*]

WARWICKSHIRE

B.R. standard class 5MT 4-6-0 No. 73099 passes Kenilworth Junction with the SLS "S.M.J.R." tour returning to Euston from Birmingham New Street on 29 April 1956.

[*T. E. Williams*]

G.W.R. "Dukedog" 4-4-0 No. 9015 approaches Stratford Old Town with the REC "South Midlander" special to Moreton-in-Marsh on 24 April 1955. [T. E. Williams

S.M.J.R. IN WARWICK- SHIRE

G.W.R. 61XX class 2-6-2T No. 6111 heads east out of Kineton with an REC special from Stratford-on-Avon, 14 September 1963. [T. E. Williams

M.R. class 3F 0-6-0 No. 43222 approaches Broom at the western end of the line, en route from Hitchin to Birmingham New Street with the SLS "S.M.J.R." tour on 29 April 1956. [T. E. Williams

The privately preserved ⯈ L.N.E.R. class B12/3 4-6-0 No. 61572 climbs away from the L.N.W.R. main line at Blisworth past Gayton Sidings with the Midland & Great Northern Joint Railway Preservation Society "Wandering 1500" rail tour from Broad Street to Stratford-on-Avon, 5 October 1963.

[*Patrick Russell*

S.R. class U 2-6-0 No. 31639 pilots class Q1 0-6-0 No. 33006 past Ettington with the HCRS "Six Counties" rail tour from Paddington to Wellingborough via Stratford-on-Avon and Leamington Spa on 7 March 1965.

⯆

[*Patrick Russell*

MORE S.M.J.R.

L.M.S. class 4F 0-6-0 No. 44188 passes the Ettington distant as it blasts up-grade through Goldicutt cutting on the outward journey from Birmingham Snow Hill to Woodford Halse with the SLS special last train over the Stratford-on-Avon & Midland Junction Railway on 24 April 1965.

[Patrick Russell

The last G.W.R. "Saint" class 4-6-0 to remain in service, No. 2920 SAINT DAVID, stands in Gloucester station on 15 June 1952 with an SLS Birmingham to Swindon special.

[T. E. Williams]

CHURCHWARD 4-6-0s

G.W.R. "Star" class 4-6-0 No. 4056 PRINCESS MARGARET approaches Shrewsbury with the 1956 TRPS special from Paddington to Towyn on 22 September.

[T. E. Williams]

M.S.W.J.R. 2-4-0 No. 1335 heads an SLS special to Shipston-on-Stour near Stretton-on-Fosse, 31 August 1952.

[*T. E. Williams*

GREAT WESTERN BYWAYS

G.W.R. 1361 class 0-6-0ST No. 1365 approaches Uffington with an REC special returning from Faringdon on 26 April 1959.

[*M. W. Earley*

G.W.R. "Dean Goods" 0-6-0 No. 2474 leaves Moreton-in-Marsh with the REC "South Midlander" special to Shipston-on-Stour, 24 April 1955.

[*T. E. Williams*

⋀

The last G.W.R. "County" class 4-6-0 No. 1011 COUNTY OF CHESTER opens up vigorously after negotiating Didcot west curve with an SLS special returning from Swindon to Birmingham, 20 September 1964.

[M. Pope

COUNTY OF CHESTER

COUNTY OF CHESTER in action again on the following weekend with the 1964 TRPS special which it hauled from Wolverhampton Low Level to Ruabon on 26 September.

⋁

[T. E. Williams

G.W.R. 1366 class 0-6-0PT No. 1366 takes the centre road through Swindon Junction with the RCTS "Swindon & Highworth" rail tour running direct from the works to Highworth, 25 April 1954.　　　[T. E. Williams

SWINDON

G.W.R. 14XX class 0-4-2T No. 1444 standing at Swindon Junction before departure for Calne with a Great Western Society tour of G.W.R. branch lines on 20 September 1964.
V　　　　　　　　[M. Pope

PENDENNIS CASTLE

G.W.R. "Castle" class 4-6-0 No. 4079 PENDENNIS CASTLE passes Reading West with the Ian Allan high-speed special from Paddington to Plymouth on 9 May 1964 to celebrate the Diamond Jubilee of CITY OF TRURO's epic run in 1904. The Castle's firebars collapsed whilst running at 96 m.p.h. near Lavington with this train and it was subsequently withdrawn from service.   [Brian Stephenson

Following its withdrawal from service PENDENNIS CASTLE was bought for private preservation and became the last steam engine to be overhauled at Swindon works. Its first run after restoration was on an Ian Allan rail tour from Paddington to Swindon via Worcester and Gloucester, and is seen climbing the final 1 in 60 up to Sapperton Tunnel on 8 August 1965.

[Brian Stephenson

LOWER LEFT: No. 4079 eases the Ian Allan "Birkenhead Flyer" under the Wolverhampton High Level–Bescot Line as it enters Wolverhampton Low Level on the down run from Didcot to Chester, 4 March 1967. This special closely followed "The Zulu" hauled by CLUN CASTLE, both trains being run from Paddington to Birkenhead to mark the end of through passenger services.

[Brian Stephenson

G.W.R. class 61XX 2-6-2T No. 6106 passes the Twyford distant as it returns from Henley-on-Thames with the LCGB–REC ''Thames Valley'' rail tour, 25 July 1965.

[*Brian Stephenson*]

G.W.R. ''Castle'' class 4-6-0 No. 5054 EARL OF DUCIE passes through Sonning cutting at speed with an Oxford University Railway Society tour from Paddington to Worcester on 16 May 1964.

[*Brian Stephenson*]

THAMES VALLEY

G.W.R. "Dukedog" 4-4-0 ≫ No. 9017 approaches Bourne End with the REC "Severn Rambler" rail tour from Windsor to Cheltenham Spa via Thame and Stow-on-the-Wold, 20 April 1958.

[J. D. Edwards

G.W.R. class 57XX 0-6-0PT No. 9773 approaches Poyle Estate Halt en route from West Drayton to Staines West with the LCGB—REC "Thames Valley" rail tour on 25 July 1965. A short stretch of this branch was being used for trials of the "wiggly-wire" system of inductive train communication. The conductors for this are clearly visible between the rails.
∨   [Patrick Russell

The prototype G.W.R. "Hall" class 4-6-0 No. 4900 SAINT MARTIN pulls out of Stratford-on-Avon with an SLS Birmingham to Swindon special on 7 September 1958.

[T. E. Williams

COLLETT 4-6-0s

G.W.R. "King" class 4-6-0 No. 6000 KING GEORGE V passes Little Somerford at 83 m.p.h. with the westbound Ian Allan "Severn & Wessex Express" from Paddington to Severn Tunnel Junction on 14 May 1960.

[R. J. Blenkinsop

G.W.R. "Grange" class 4-6-0 No. 6859 YIEWSLEY GRANGE leaves Johnston on the last lap to Milford Haven with the RCTS–SLS "Last Steam Train to West Wales" on 26 September 1965.   [M. Brian Rutherford

The Great Western Society's G.W.R. "Manor" class 4-6-0 No. 7808 COOKHAM MANOR leaves Whitehouse Farm Tunnel, between High Wycombe and Beaconsfield, with their special train from Birmingham for the Taplow Open Day, 17 September 1966.   [M. Pope

DEVON AND CORNWALL

G.W.R. 28XX class 2-8-0 No. 2887 toils up the steep ascent of Rattery bank with the Plymouth Railway Circle—RCTS ''Cornubian'' rail tour westbound from Exeter to Plymouth and Penzance on 3 May 1964.

[Peter F. Bowles

≪ G.W.R. 1366 class 0-6-0PT No. 1369 pauses in Dunmere Woods with the PRC "Wenford Special" celebrating 130 years of steam on the Wenford Bridge line, 19 September 1964.   [J. C. Haydon

L.M.S. Ivatt class 2MT 2-6-2Ts Nos. 41206 & 41291 take water at Torrington before returning to Barnstaple with the RCTS–PRC "Exmoor Ranger" tour on 27 March 1965.   [R. A. Panting
∨

G.W.R. 57XX class 0-6-0PT No. 4624 waits at Easton before returning to Melcombe Regis with the RCTS "Wessex Wyvern" rail tour on 8 July 1956.   [J. Spencer Gilks

Sunset on the Bridport branch with L.M.S. Ivatt class 2MT 2-6-2Ts Nos. 41301 & 41284 (at the rear of the train) climbing slowly towards Powerstock with the LCGB "Dorset Belle" rail tour on the return journey to Maiden Newton, 27 February 1966.
∇   [Brian Stephenson

DORSET

B.R. standard class 4MT 2-6-4T No. 80146 nears Worgret Junction with the RCTS "Farewell to Southern Steam" rail tour returning from Swanage to Wareham, 18 June 1967. [*Patrick Russell*]

L.M.S. Ivatt class 2MT 2-6-2T No. 41298 proceeds cautiously through the streets of Weymouth on its way to the Channel Islands Quay with the LCGB "Green Arrow" rail tour on 3 July 1966. [*Brian Stephenson*]

SOMERSET AND DORSET

S. & D.J.R. class 7F 2-8-0 No. 53807 pounds up the 1 in 50 gradient to Devonshire Tunnel on the climb out of Bath Green Park with the Ian Allan "Severn & Wessex Express" bound for Bournemouth West on 14 May 1960.

[*R. J. Blenkinsop*]

G.W.R. 2251 class 0-6-0 ≫ No. 3210 waits at Highbridge with the LCGB "Somerset & Dorset" rail tour on its return journey from Burnham-on-Sea to Evercreech Junction, 30 September 1962. [Patrick Russell

L.M.S. class 8F 2-8-0 No. 48309 approaches Chilcompton on the long climb through the Mendips to Masbury Summit with the repeat LCGB "Wessex Downsman" rail tour en route from Bath Green Park to Bournemouth West on 2 May 1965. [Patrick Russell ∨

L.M.S. class 2MT 2-6-2Ts Nos. 41307 & 41283 leave Glastonbury for Highbridge with the LCGB ''Mendip Merchantman'' rail tour on 1 January 1966. This should have been the last day of service on the S.& D., but the closure was postponed for two months owing to licensing difficulties with the replacement 'bus services.

[S. C. Nash

SOMERSET AND DORSET FINALE

S.R. ''West Country'' & ''Battle of Britain'' class 4-6-2s Nos. 34006 BUDE & 34057 BIGGIN HILL climb the 1 in 50 between Devonshire Tunnel and Combe Down Tunnel with the LCGB ''Somerset & Dorset'' rail tour southbound from Bath to Bournemouth on the last day of service, 5 March 1966. [Brian Stephenson

On the Sunday following the end of services the SLS ran a special last train from Bath Green Park to Bourne-mouth Central and back. L.M.S. class 8F 2-8-0 No. 48706 and B.R. standard class 4MT 2-6-4T No. 80043 coast downgrade from Combe Down Tunnel past the site of Midford goods depot on the outward journey on 6 March 1966.   [Brian Stephenson

B.R. standard class 3MT 2-6-0 No. 77014 runs into Spetisbury with the LCGB "Hants & Dorset" rail tour returning from Blandford Forum to Broadstone over the truncated remains of the Somerset and Dorset line, 16 October 1966.   [Brian Stephenson

GOSPORT BRANCH

Λ
S.R. Class N 2-6-0 No. 31411 pulls strongly away from
Fort Brockhurst level-crossing on its return from Gosport
to Fareham with the Southern Counties Touring Society
"Southdown Venturer" on 20 February 1966.

[Patrick Russell

L.S.W.R. class H15 ⋙ 4-6-2T No. 30516 after arrival at Fawley with the LCGB ''South Western Limited'' on 18 September 1960. [Patrick Russell]

S.R. Class USA 0-6-0Ts Nos. 30064 and 30069 approach Frost Lane Crossing on the return journey from Fawley with the LCGB ''Hampshire Branch Lines'' rail tour on 9 April 1967. ⩔ [Brian Stephenson]

FAWLEY BRANCH

BULLEID ENGINES

S.R. "West Country" class 4-6-2s Nos. 34023 BLACKMORE VALE and 34108 WINCANTON climb to Bincombe Tunnel with the RCTS "Farewell to Southern Steam" rail tour on 18 June 1967 returning from Weymouth to Salisbury via Eastleigh.
[Patrick Russell

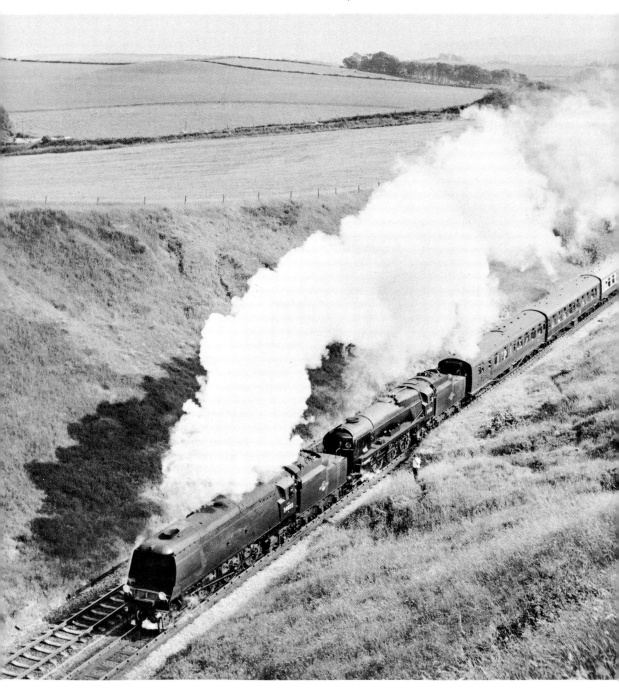

UPPER RIGHT:
S.R. class Q1 0-6-0s Nos. 33027 & 33006 restart from Baynards with the LCGB "Wealdsman" rail tour, 13 June 1965, the last train over the Horsham-Guildford line.   [Patrick Russell

CENTRE RIGHT:
S.R. "Modified West Country" class 4-6-2 No. 34042 DOR-CHESTER approaches Vauxhall from Waterloo with a Lyons "Zoom" special on 30 August 1964.   [Brian Stephenson

LOWER RIGHT:
S.R. "Merchant Navy" class 4-6-2 No. 35005 CANADIAN PACIFIC skirts Salisbury Plain near Warminster as it heads for Swindon with a WRS special, 23 May 1965.   [Brian Stephenson

B.R. standard class 4MT 4-6-0 No. 75070 leaving Southampton Terminus for Fareham with the RCTS "Solent" rail tour on 20 March 1966.
[Patrick Russell

SOUTHAMPTON

Another view of the RCTS "Solent" rail tour of 20 March 1966 with S.R. USA class 0-6-0Ts Nos. 30073 & 30064 getting a clear road through Southampton Central on their non-stop run from the Terminus station to Fawley. *[Patrick Russell*
∨

L.S.W.R. class B4 0-4-0T No. 30096 leaves the Docks with the second LCGB "B4 Dock Tank" rail tour on 6 April 1963.

[R. A. Panting

S.R. "Merchant Navy" class 4-6-2 No. 35028 CLAN LINE skirts the River Itchen as it heads north for Waterloo past St. Denys on 2 July 1967 with the B.R. Southern Region "Farewell to Steam" special train returning from Bournemouth.

[Brian Stephenson

The preserved L.S.W.R. class T9 4-4-0 No. 120 waits to leave Waterloo with the LCGB "Sussex Coast Limited" rail tour on 24 June 1962, bound for Horsham via Effingham Junction and Guildford, on its first run after restoration.

[Brian Stephenson

WATERLOO

S.R. class U 2-6-0s Nos. 31791 & 31639 back onto their train at Waterloo for the repeat run of the RCTS "Longmoor" rail tour on 30 April 1966.

[Brian Stephenson

L.S.W.R. class 02 0-4-4Ts Nos. 24 CALBOURNE & 31 CHALE leave Brading on the return from Shanklin to Ryde Esplanade with the LCGB "Isle of Wight Steam Farewell" rail tour on the last day of steam operation in the Island, 31 December 1966.
[*John H. Bird*

ISLAND FAREWELLS

L.B.S.C.R. "Terrier" class A1X 0-6-0Ts Nos. 32636 and 32670 (at the rear of the train) cross Langston Bridge to Hayling Island with the LCGB "Hayling Farewell" rail tour, the last train over the branch from Havant on 3 November 1963.
[*Brian Stephenson*

L.S.W.R. class 02 0-4-4T No. 30200 and L.B.S.C.R. class E1 0-6-0T No. 32694 at Droxford before returning to Fareham with the LCGB "Solent Limited" rail tour on 30 April 1961. [Patrick Russell

L.S.W.R. class T9 4-4-0s Nos. 30301 & 30732 leave West Meon, with the last through run over the Meon Valley line, returning to Waterloo with the RCTS "Hampshireman" on 6 February 1955.
[E. C. Griffith

HAMPSHIRE BYWAYS

⚠

The last S.R. class S15 4-6-0 No. 30837 hammers its way up Medstead bank en route for Eastleigh with the LCGB "S15 Commemorative" rail tour on 9 January 1966. This tour was so heavily booked that it ran on two successive Sundays. This is the relief train which ran on the first Sunday.

[Patrick Russell]

S.R. class U 2-6-0 No. 31639 brings the LCGB "S15 Commemorative" rail tour back from Bordon to Bentley on 9 January 1966, where S15 No. 30837 was waiting to take over. The train is seen soon after leaving Bordon.

[Brian Stephenson]

⚡

LONGMOOR
MILITARY RAILWAY

Army Dept. 2-10-0 No. 600 GORDON makes light of the climb to Haslemere as it heads the repeat RCTS "Longmoor" rail tour of 30 April 1966 from Woking to Liss.
[M. Pope

UPPER RIGHT: Army Dept. Hunslet 0-6-0ST No. 195 and GORDON pass Liss Forest with the same RCTS special on 30 April 1966 as they make their way over L.M.R. metals from Liss to Longmoor Downs.
[Patrick Russell

Army Dept. Hunslet 0-6-0ST No. 196 returns to Longmoor Downs after traversing the Hollywater loop with the RCTS "Longmoor" rail tour on 30 April 1966. The locomotive had started so many fires as a result of the dry hot weather that it was replaced by a diesel locomotive for a second circuit of the loop. ≫
[Brian Stephenson

≪ Adams class 0395 0-6-0 No. 30577 leaves Eastleigh on 8 May 1954 with the REC "Southampton Docks" tour returning to Farnborough. [L. Elsey

Adams class 0415 4-4-2 radial tank No. 30582 starts its short train from well back inside Waterloo station and the REC "L.S.W.R. Suburban" rail tour gets under way, 19 March 1961. [Patrick Russell
∨

L.S.W.R. VETERANS

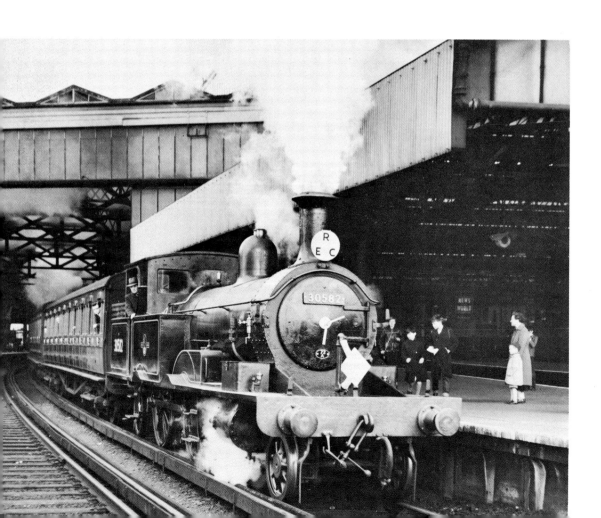

Drummond class 700 0-6-0 No. 30339 stands at the disused Ludgate Hill station between Holborn Viaduct and Blackfriars awaiting departure for Ascot with the LCGB "South Western Limited" rail tour on 18 September 1960. [Patrick Russell

Beattie class 0298 2-4-0 well-tanks Nos. 30585 & 30587 set off from Surbiton for Hampton Court with the RCTS–SLS "South Western Suburban" rail tour on 2 December 1962. The great success of this tour made certain of a repeat two weeks later. [Patrick Russell

SURREY

The last L.S.W.R. class M7 0-4-4T No. 30053 climbs towards Chipstead en route from Purley to Tattenham Corner with the LCGB ''Surrey Wanderer'' rail tour on 5 July 1964. No. 30053 is now preserved in the U.S.A. at the Steamtown Foundation, Bellows Falls, Virginia.

[*Brian Stephenson*

L.S.W.R. class L12 4-4-0 No. 30434 near Ash Green on its way to Tongham with the REC "Hants & Surrey" rail tour, 26 September 1953. This train ran from Farnborough to Bordon via Guildford for a visit to the Longmoor Military Railway.

[S. C. Nash

L.S.W.R. class H16 4-6-2T No. 30517 heads the repeat RCTS–SLS "South Western Suburban" rail tour from Wimbledon to Chessington South as it approaches Malden Manor on 16 December 1962.

[Patrick Russell

S.R. "King Arthur" class N15 4-6-0 No. 30796 SIR DODINAS LE SAVAGE sets out from Brighton for Victoria on the last stage of the RCTS "Brighton Atlantic Farewell" rail tour on 13 April 1955. [*S. C. Nash*]

MAUNSELL 4-6-0s

S.R. "Remembrance" class N15X 4-6-0 No. 32329 STEPHENSON leaves Andover Junction for Waterloo on 8 July 1956 with the RCTS "Wessex Wyvern". [*R. C. Riley*]

⚠ The last S.R. "Lord Nelson" class 4-6-0 No. 30861 LORD ANSON emerges from Buckhorn Weston Tunnel on its magnificent farewell run from Exeter Central to Salisbury with the SCTS "South Western Limited" of 2 September 1962.
[G. A. Richardson

S.R. class S15 4-6-0 No. 30839 heads the RCTS–LCGB "Midhurst Belle" near Virginia Water on its way to Woking via Ascot, 18 October 1964.
[R. A. Lissenden
⚠

B.R. standard class 4 2-6-4T No. 80145 crosses the Thames at Kingston with the LCGB's one hundredth rail tour, the "South Western Suburban", on 5 February 1967 en route from Wimbledon to Shepperton.

[*Brian Stephenson*]

SOUTHERN SUBURBAN

B.R. standard class 5 4-6-0 No. 73022 passes West Croydon with the SCTS "Southern Wanderer" from Victoria to Templecombe via Dorking North, Fareham and Bournemouth on 28 March 1965.   [*Brian Stephenson*]

B.R. standard class 2 2-6-0 No. 78038 approaches Crystal Palace Low Level with the LCGB "Surrey Wanderer" rail tour on 5 July 1964, while running tender first between Tulse Hill and Beckenham Junction. [Brian Stephenson]

L.M.S. Ivatt class 2MT 2-6-0 No. 46509 passes Streatham with the LCGB–REC "Thames Valley" rail tour whilst travelling from Waterloo to Kensington Olympia via Teddington, East Putney and Norwood Junction on 25 July 1965.
[Patrick Russell]

L.B.S.C.R. class C2X 0-6-0 No. 32543 approaches Tulse Hill with the empty stock of the "John Milton Special" ramblers' excursion from Crystal Palace Low Level to Chesham on 3 June 1956.   [R. C. Riley

L.B.S.C.R. class H2 4-4-2 No. 32425 TREVOSE HEAD enters West Croydon with an SLS special from Victoria to Portsmouth on 3 May 1953.   [S. C. Nash

BRIGHTON ENGINES

L.B.S.C.R. class K 2-6-0 No. 32353 at speed near Partridge Green with the RCTS "Sussex Coast" rail tour returning from Brighton to London Bridge via Horsham on 7 October 1962. [M. Pope

L.B.S.C.R. class A1X 0-6-0T No. 32636 pilots class E6 0-6-2T No. 32418 with the RCTS "Sussex Coast" rail tour as they climb through Falmer station on the way from Brighton to Seaford, 7 October 1962. [M. Pope

L.B.S.C.R. class E5X 0-6-2Ts Nos. 32576 & 32570 arrive at Midhurst from Pulborough with the RCTS ''Hampshireman'' on 6 February 1955. They are about to make the last journey over the Midhurst–Petersfield line.

[*E. C. Griffith*

WEST SUSSEX

S.R. class Q 0-6-0 No. 30530 speeds down the Mid-Sussex line towards Billingshurst with the RCTS–LCGB ''Midhurst Belle'' rail tour bound for Midhurst from Horsham on 18 October 1964.

[*Mrs. Michaeles Stephenson*

Captain W. G. Smith's preserved G.N.R. class J52 0-6-0ST No. 1247 arrives at Horsted Keynes after reversal at Haywards Heath with the "Blue Belle" special from London Bridge to Sheffield Park on 1 April 1962.

[*Brian Stephenson*

BLUE BELLE

Bluebell railway L.S.W.R. Adams 4-4-2T No. 488 and L.B.S.C.R. class E4 0-6-2T No. 473 BIRCH GROVE approach Ardingly with the "Blue Belle" special of 15 September 1963, en route from Haywards Heath to Sheffield Park. [*Brian Stephenson*

S.E.C.R. class D1 4-4-0 No. 31545 awaits departure from Victoria for a non-stop run to Margate on 19 May 1957 with the SLS "Chatham & Dover" special. The 4-4-0 was driven by the famous driver Sammy Gingell who can be seen standing on the platform, and the train became known as "The Gingell Belle".

[S. C. Nash

SOUTH EASTERN

S.E.C.R. class 01 0-6-0 No. 31258 at Shepherd's Well with an REC special touring the East Kent Railway, 23 May 1959. The van conveyed bicycles for passengers inspecting the locomotives at Betteshanger Colliery.

[R. C. Riley

S.E.C.R. class 01 0-6-0 No. 31065 and class C 0-6-0 No. 31592 wait at Paddock Wood to take over the LCGB "South Eastern Limited" for the last journey over the Hawkhurst branch on 11 June 1961. [Patrick Russell

S.R. "King Arthur" class 4-6-0 No. 30782 SIR BRIAN waits for the road at Margate with the LCGB "Kentish Venturer" rail tour run to mark the end of steam on the South Eastern Division of the Southern Region, 25 February 1962. [Brian Stephenson

≪ L.N.E.R. class A3 4-6-2 No. 4472 FLYING SCOTSMAN is seen on arrival at Kings Cross with a Lyons "Zoom" special from York, 30 August 1964.
[*Brian Stephenson*

NIGHT ARRIVALS

The last steam locomotive built for British Railways at Swindon Works, standard class 9F 2-10-0 No. 92220 EVENING STAR at Paddington after arrival with an Ian Allan rail tour from Eastleigh on 3 April 1964.
∨   [*Brian Stephenson*